Primitive Mood

WINNER OF THE
2009 T. S. ELIOT PRIZE

The T. S. Eliot Prize for Poetry is an annual award sponsored by Truman State University Press for the best unpublished book-length collection of poetry in English, in honor of native Missourian T. S. Eliot's considerable intellectual and artistic legacy.

Judge for 2009: Virgil Suárez

Primitive Mood

David Moolten

Truman State University Press
New Odyssey Series

Published by Truman State University Press, Kirksville, Missouri USA
tsup.truman.edu
© 2009 David Moolten
New Odyssey Series
All rights reserved

Cover image: details from XXXXIIII Sol (Trumpfkarte des Mantegna-Tarots), 15th century. Florenz, Uffizi, Gabinetto Disegni e Stampe.

Cover design: Teresa Wheeler
Type: Arno Pro © Adobe Systems Inc.; Galahad © Adobe Systems Inc.
Printed by: Thomson Shore, Dexter, Michigan USA

Library of Congress Cataloging-in-Publication Data

Moolten, David, 1961–
Primitive mood / David Moolten.
    p. cm.
Winner of the 2009 T. S. Eliot Prize for Poetry.
ISBN 978-1-931112-94-9 (hardback : alk. paper) — ISBN 978-1-931112-95-6 (pbk. : alk. paper)
I. Title.
PS3563.O5539P75 2009
811'.54—dc22

                                                                              2009025251

The paper in this publication meets or exceeds the minimum requirements of the American National Standard for Information Sciences—Permanence of Paper for Printed Library Materials, ANSI Z39.48–1992.

For the children

Contents

III

Acknowledgments

My thanks to the editors of the following publications in which these poems first appeared:

American Scholar: "Magic"
American Literary Review: "Lorca in Harlem, 1929"
Chelsea: "Portrait"
EPOCH: "Cinderella," "Glass"
Exquisite Corpse: "Cargo Cult," "Contagion,"
    "Groundless and Still Believed," "Expatriate"
Georgia Review: "Klezmer"
Kenyon Review: "Golem"
Many Mountains Moving: "Rushmore"
Ploughshares: "Beauty," "The Red Shoes"
Poetry: "Dybbuk"
Poetry International: "Lorca's Grave," "Miners"
Poetry Northwest: "Fiddle"
Prairie Schooner: "Boy Raised by Wolves," "The Girl
    Without Hands," "Sleeping Beauty"
The Journal: "Prodigal," "Rape of the Sabine Women,"
    "Tolerance"
Sewanee Review: "Easter, 1930"
Shenandoah: "Columbarium," "Parable of the Capsized
    Canoe"
Southern Review: "Photograph of Mass Grave
    Unearthed, Rwanda," "Story," "Soup," "Tristan,"
    "Yellow Star"
Southwest Review: "Aperture"
West Branch: "Bomber at the Museum," "Medusa"

I

The Girl Without Hands

Living is so endless, a fairy tale
Bluntly cuts away the surplus, leaving
Just the odd detail, the stingy bone. Who knows
What story she tells to explain herself
That night he finds her eating in his orchard
Like a child bobbing for apples, a tall axe
Of a man just like her father when he stood
Over her in that dark room of his house,
Of a world she can't grasp, only behold?
Stories manipulate, change everything.
But she has nothing to lose, the hands
Like a lady's elegant white gloves
Already misplaced. Of course he wants her
Though she's cold and pale to the touch, her whole
Body a stump, a voice remote from its words.
He gives her hands of silver, his upon her
However gentle just compensation,
Precious metal, the clumsiest compassion
Compared with what she must feel. But the son
She bears by the name of *Sorrowful*
Brims with her own blood, no prosthesis growing
Out of her. Only then do her born with hands
Return like fruit, love an extremity
Like a lizard's tail or the legs of a starfish
Mindless in its shallow glittering pool.
The boy maims her again into beauty;
Becomes her tenuous appendage, gone
The numbness, palpable the memory of sensation,
What she feared most, the phantom pain
And hellish pleasure. She's healed or so
The story says, writing off the devil
Who plagued her for no reason other

Than her purity. Then the man blunders in
The secret cottage and takes her in his arms,
Undoes her blouse because oh God, he's missed her;
The burden at last lifted but not really.

Boy Raised by Wolves

Not the pack's socialized carnage or yowls
Of mercy in the wild child's gut-wrenching story,
But North 10th Street, a boy crouched against a dog
On the kitchen's stained tiles, his packed bag
In the hands of the caseworker there to save him
By rending him away. It's a lick in the face
That comes closest to fostering love
Not the system's forest of bureaucracy
Or the door slam of his late mother's sister
Back from cleaning up other people's messes
In hotels to smoke in her robe at the blinds
Furiously high. It's her gimpy stray
Of just as humble pedigree, a bitch,
As she's called without contempt, who smelled trouble,
Crept off the torn couch as when the muscled
Boyfriend returned ten seconds after leaving
For his stash, her ears down, her forbearing eyes more
Human than sentient, Samuel Johnson's dog
Of despair which Goya painted in a last
Nameless mural, yearning from a sickly
Brown pinnacle of earth, the whole world
The chain that holds her back. If this boy drew
On his blank cracked plaster he'd get what he gets
Anyway too many nights according to the state.
Her he won't, a trifle of sticks and bones
He'll outgrow into a mean, aloof maturity.
But right now they're fused together, adhere
Like paint and wall, peering over the brink
At the rest of their days, no instinct for how
The worst happens for good reason. Housebroken,
Dumbly loyal, she lets him have his brief
Handful of fur, lets him bury his head
In her side, in that primitive mood, grief.

The Escape

The murderer at the knee-high kindergarten table
Is this proud boy's father and a calm abides
In his scrutiny, gazing back from the show-
And-tell drawing. He's crude, an impulsive snarl
Of streaks, a stick figure stick-up man
In magenta and forest green, accurate
For the enormous house with its shiny gate
Where correction means another kind
Of fix because the walls work both ways.
But it doesn't matter. He passes through
Plexiglas and reinforced steel, most of everything
Space, inside or between, as with atoms
Or people, adamant distance, vague eyes
When spoken to. He smiles as only a child
Could picture, radiant as the spoked wheel sun,
Nothing wrong from the standpoint of perspective
Or proportion, such idle worship per se,
Just the line that separates same from same
In the shadow of absence, the sentence
That begins on a child's lips, *my name is*
And ends with what crayon shows the world
He'll become, already locked inside
Like a man there's no keeping it from.

Prodigal

The bullet has no judgment, passing through
The school bus's thin skin, his vinyl
Seat back before rending his heart, a boy
Who'd almost made it to his flaking porch,
The mildly nagging note by the Cheerios box,
Almost to eighteen and gone off, guilty
Of none of the usual, no TV
Lifted from a busted-in warehouse,
No signature spray-painted on bridges,
No air-venting flick of the syringe, no addiction
Except by them to his simple resonance,
Dancing, talking, laughing, and surely
No 9 mm, short recoil, double action,
Fired from a screeching Camry's half-down
Tinted window, a boy who rebelled, betrayed
Everyone's expectations with ok grades,
Who could think, so that they thought they could save him
Little by little, day by day, like coupons,
Maybe they the recidivists, the stubborn
Perpetuators and purveyors of calamity,
Prodigal to even have a son.

Sleeping Beauty

Six months on the street, she's one long swoon
Into loathsomeness, soiled jeans jacket, bits
Of city park sycamore leaves, a touch
Of forest embellishing her hair, no milk
Carton runaway, booze the none-too-magic
But just as toxic curse, half a fifth in one
Dared swig, her companions yelling, slapping her face.
And the hero? He jogs in the same grass
But another world, has a sales meeting
In an hour, never his ambition to happen
On a comatose girl. But here she lies
In wait for his strange, impartial lips,
Hers already parted, a cold ring of spit,
No tongue, just breath after noble breath
Mingled with hard thrusts between her breasts,
The rescue flawless, by the book and at last
She rebuffs him with her weak cough. By then
A small audience sputters applause and he smiles,
Heady with the fleeting magnanimity.
What comes next now that she has a pulse
He can't tell, never taught group homes or dollar
Tricks behind the Greyhound station on mannequins
At the Red Cross. Helpless except to kiss her,
He did, trembly and proud, thinking he saved her,
He saved her. But the story's still not over.

The Red Shoes

Pulling out government coupons for the first time
In a Kroger twelve blocks from her walk up
So the bagboys and cashiers and seniors
Browsing tabloids would all be strangers,
She's slow motion through and past their stares.
She feels every nuance of her body
As a tense repressed trembling, a calculated,
Conscious stepping, just as much a dance
Of desperation as that solo waltz
Around the brass pole in the gentleman's club
She'd never do. Nothing said, but the gist
Of the story bared, Lonnie gone and the car
After missed payments, no degree, nurses aide
Not enough for even store brand soup,
And those looks from everyone contribute
To the scrutiny she's already put herself under,
The wondering what's become of her
Least dashed hope, like that man in the dominion
Of his cubicle at the welfare office
Teasing out the names of men who stayed
The night. She's been made small. She's been cut down
To size like that little girl with the red shoes
Told by the angel she'd dance for all
The vain children, dance through the moonlight
And the villages and the dark dreamy woods,
Who never stopped even when she stood begging
The executioner not to lop off her head,
Then letting him harvest her feet instead.
So she seasons her sauce with damp salt
From her own eyes and her back to her son
In his proud sneakers and best sullen thirteen
Because he won't ever know she's good

As dirt, a polite little clot of nothing
Waiting while that laughing bureaucrat
Carried on in front of her long and personal
On the phone. *Approved* was the word he used,
Meaning yes to those two sacks which would last
However long they must like the whole
Brutal fiction of grace, the executioner
Giving the girl crutches after the axe.

Beauty

He entered the sty, and she cringed. She'd always
Remember him, a beast with black hair
And blue eyes, a young German, and the sound
Of screeching ducks and gunshots in the barnyard
Where treacherous neighbors had gossiped
Away the good frightened family who'd stashed her
And hers like livestock with souls, butchered then
Or driven off in a truck. Comprehending
Her face, his rifle still trained, he lowered
His stare to the straw-laced mud. He left,

And with this beautiful act became like a pig
That had swallowed a diamond: whoever
Slit him open would wonder where it came from.
She knew what she rarely said afterwards,
That he looked like a boy she could have liked,
Like the tall coachman who let her ride
With the crates once on his flat wagon
Or the rabbi's son she'd daydreamed kissing
In the lilacs behind the gymnasium, a real prince
At whom she could never so much as smile
Without having her decency questioned …

And so the curse is lifted, the one
Who sprayed their blood in the usual ritual
All over the rotted stoop hasn't urged them
To kneel in his grunting, accurate tongue
Because he's in here with her and in love,
Transformed by it, if only for an instant.

Cinderella

Among Oswiciem's vast heaps of shoes luck
Has left one of yours on top so that you,
Whoever you were, become the absence
Which blossoms from it, the girl for whom one seeks
Fitting thoughts or words. Forget the rot
Which has alchemized a vague gray from blue or beige,
Easy to imagine its mate, perfect opposite
Like a lover, still clinging to your foot
As the story would insist, that you jolted
From here holding up a gown's dainty flounces
While clopping through the sullen woods, spurned
The barracks and faux showers, the industrial hearths.
So any notion of identity or restitution
Might reduce to juvenile romance, a prince
In search of a shy, mistreated debutante,
When everyone knows the other lies elsewhere
In those piles with its Jewish sole, that after you
Emerged ragged and shorn, they ordered women
To kneel and sift, picking out the best.
Perhaps they missed yours, or hadn't yet
Got to them. But others just like them
Might have ridden a train back to the world
So that a Fräulein in Stuttgart in 1944
Could probe with her curious toes a snug pump
With a modest heel her mother has received
In a bundle of government surplus.
And this stepsister of sorts, maybe she doesn't appear
Cruel or ugly, doesn't even know when she waltzes
About her kitchen to Strauss from the radio
And waits for her beau, for the war to end,
How readily a person becomes a metonym,
A hat, a ring, a shoe, transferable, interchangeable,

How only the truth retains its magic fidelity
Like a glass slipper worn by a girl of cinders
And smoke, impossibly fragile and lost for good.

Yellow Star

He saved it like a captured butterfly,
A medal decorating a box of yellowed black
And white snapshots, a souvenir of his first
Lost life, infernal and exquisite, a flared match
His hand could tolerate just a moment.
Up close it looked imperfect, homespun, fringed
With strands from the coat off which he'd torn it
The day the war ended, the long-discarded coat
On which she slowly, carefully sewed
What she'd cut from cloth. Posted on walls
The edict said everyone must make their own,
Arbitrary and specific as any
In Leviticus, in the Torah that made him
Who he was, a noxious star, a hexagram,
Petaled like a sunflower, a saffron dahlia,
A bloom she might have pinned to his lapel
Were they going out to waltz. Maybe that's why
He kept it, as a mnemonic of her
Ordinary, singular soul, which imbued
Whatever her fingers touched, made it
Less horrific, less contemptible
Like the apple had Eve grown the tree herself
And the two of them stood before it scared
And hungry. Despite his teaching, her shift
In a shoe factory, they'd little to eat
With the rationing in Zagreb, no garden,
Not even a window box for their apartment,
Just bricks and dust, a candle in the glass
And the kiss it betokened, not much but savored
In a way that anywhere before became paradise
And this the flower he left with.

Columbarium

dovecote (Latin)

Legend says doves saved the Altneu synagogue
In Prague in 1558, really
Angels in disguise who hovered cooing
Along the roof while the ghetto burned.
You can imagine the faint creak as their wings fanned
The flames away from Europe's oldest shul
The obdurate roost of tradition
After each purge, but not why children
Never felt the same blessed shuddering
When the Germans stoked their kilns at Terezin.
The ancient poor called themselves lucky
In Rome to have if not an ornate tomb
For the body then a small hole in the wall
For its residue in a row of such holes,
In a stack of such rows, like the better off
For their birds. In 1944 those children
Not yet ash stood as in a fire line and passed
Box after box from the shed with the arched doors
And tired brick, a spur track to the river,
The Russian tanks getting close. Perhaps
There never was a way to contain such truth.
Though as they scattered handfuls of gray silt
To cloud and clot the current they must
Have fluttered a little, carried in the wind
As when a flock is released and wheels
With calm restraint over a city's spires and eaves
Before returning to its niches. The humble
In the ancient temple sacrificed pigeons
Instead of lambs on the altar, all
They could afford for their burnt offering,
Their holocaust, Greek from Hebrew, the word *olah*

Meaning *that which goes up*. Perhaps when you stand
In the synagogue on a Friday night
Once the crowds disperse, listening to the past
Quietly murmured in a dead language
You are that small opening, that repository
Of memory, which is its own homing
Crossing the impossible distance like a dove.

Story

A man exiles himself from himself, flip-flops
Hemispheres, Berlin for Buenos Aires,
As if the backwards swirl of water
In the sink could reverse the course
Of his life. He leaves the black castle oozing smoke
From a fir-stippled clearing of snow
For a white cottage that overlooks the beach
Like a conch hurled up among the cypress
And hermits there, venturing forth
Only in the cool of dusk. He prefers
The end, the denouement, the fading out,
Having traded the first half of this most
Bloody century for the last. That is the story
His wife refuses to believe, the one
She has heard but claims not to know,
A story which stalks him across the slant light
Of years like his own long shadow
On the veranda, an evil twin with a past
Who stares in their windows. Questioned, attacked
As crazy, the story has traveled far,
Has grown old just getting here. But at night,
The story dreams in a made-up tongue
Not unlike Yiddish, full of fustian
And folly, dreams of a forest where
The living names of the dead, small, but shining
With truth, cry out like stars, someplace
Terrible and distant as the bottom
Of the sea. Heaving awake, the story
Walks outside among the palm trees,
Each of which, when touched, becomes a person
Stooped in grief. Tonight, when the man hummed
In the kitchen with his wife, the story

17

Felt hands clapped across its ears
Like parentheses on a tombstone. Tonight,
When they ate codfish and green bananas
Fried and dipped in sauce, the story starved.
Tonight, when the man caressed her cheek,
The story staggered, struck across the face.
In prayers, the man forgives himself, and others
Condemn the story. But at the end
Of the story, the man dies, unpunished, yes,
But forgotten, while the story, which always
Involved the innocent, goes on, unchanged,
Speaking the unspeakable, because memory too
Is justice, nothing more than words
In the name of justice, telling this.

Soup

Anyone else would have looked like she felt
Two feet tall had you walked in on her plucking
What remained of a chicken from the garbage
But not my father's ancient already hunched up aunt.
Instead, unflappable, she chewed us out for squandering
The wondrous carcass that one should gnaw on
Or scavenge for parts with which to engineer
The concoction she soon had stirring in a pot,
Gizzards and grease, a dab of horseradish
And kosher salt, her recipe for polite excuses
And pruning faces at what we feared more
Than cow's tongue or chopped liver. She was frugal,
A *karger*, fulfilling the less-than-generous stereotype
Though mostly with herself, housed always
In a scrubby floral dress when at the door
She welcomed each of us with a crisp dollar
Or a butterscotch candy from the jar
In her larder. She treated the modern world
As her endlessly sighed-over pogrom
With its blaring appliances and disobeyed traditions,
Time alone a forced exodus, a rushed immigration
For a woman who'd spent forty years
In the same junk cramped apartment. She too
Was a leftover, a squat vat of garbled English
And malapropisms, of dire stories about boots
With a sound like cracking ribs, of towns lost
To mist and their own queer ways. She force-fed us
The crazy logic of her existence, primordial
As the swill that floated above her gas flame.
What else but bones did she have to hold onto?
Where had the Russia of her childhood gone
Except to bland photos of the handsome dead

She yanked back from oblivion to her bosom?
What could she do but hoard the past, fiercely
Cautious with her grief like a stoic, conserving
As she did for soup the leftover fat, the schmaltz
Caked in a pan, this the ritual with sentiment,
So as not to waste a succulent bit?

Tristan

It's poison seeping from his radio,
The music he'd rather die than hear
Which reminds me most of my grandfather,
How at the first strains without lifting
His yarmulke-covered head
From his book, he made it a point
In front of us to rout Wagner
The proto-Nazi, Wagner the arrogant jingoist
By quietly switching stations.
Like Tristan whose very name means heartache
My grandfather put his faith in principle,
Jilted Isolde and her sweet soprano,
And like Tristan his fidelity wavered,
I who caught him out on the porch
Humming badly along the night he thought
Everyone asleep upstairs. He murmured
As one might in an incantation or prayer,
The princess a potion for his widowed ears,
Irresistible, or just her voice rising
Over his self-ostracizing wall.
Some heroically mortal part of him
Broke down that wall and his own commandment,
Broke his heart again back into a heart.
Listening now I do more than forgive
His compromise, I miss him
Telling me about the prophets and the scribes,
Why never to get in a Volkswagen
But also his hand fine-tuning my hair.
And the opera Twain said would have been good
Without the vocal parts? That I find slow
And overwrought, though it doesn't take much
To make me surrender, enough in one cracked whisper.

Klezmer

"and he began to play over again, so that the Jew
had to jump higher than ever, and scraps of his
coat were left hanging"
—From *The Jew Among Thorns*, the
Brothers Grimm

You have fleeced people often enough, claims
The fiddler, commencing his brutal concert
On a roadside in Prussia or old Ukraine,
Music so gripping, so moving, the man
He's teasing, having fun with, can't resist
Dancing in the underbrush until he's naked
And gasping, excoriated by roses.
It's a lie of course, blood libel, a fairy tale
To tell children so they go to sleep
In fear of witches or monsters or people
Who get the better of them, mainly through lies.
A violin is just wood and catgut but cunning
In its persuasion; no instrument comes
Closer to the human voice, such exquisite wailing,
And when a klezmer troubadour strokes his,
He almost sounds that good, tunes so forlorn
They scratch at you, so jubilant they leave you
Giddy as sparkling wine. My grandfather played
For me only his stereo, the Epstein brothers,
An old record, the past scarred and warped
And repeating itself. But even he,
A staid man, a learned man would rise helpless
Like someone jerked around on strings in a story
By someone else. He'd nod and tap his shoe,
A whole village in his veins, hoofing
On their cloven feet, spinning and dropping
Knees bent, still kicking at the scraped-out strains.

So one tormented soul torments another
With his own polka, his own waltz, the breathless
Urge to celebrate what was endured;
Even now I'm greedy to hear more.

Dybbuk

Out on the porch, my grandparents performed
The exorcism, laying out the tea service
And the kugel, incredulous, confronting
My father to save him, though gently, only
In the spirit of polite conversation
Questioning what possessed him
To bring home a Puerto Rican shiksa. She knelt
In their garden, captivating and accursed
As a demon invoked by candlelit cabalists,
A far-fetched folktale straight out of Poland.
They patronized her saints, kibitzed her English,
Praying he'd see his folly, that they'd get her
Out of his system. But they might as well
Have bleated an old ram horn and recited
In the backwards tongue as denied her
To him. She hung on against all judgment. Her soul
Cohabited with his even as she devoutly
Wouldn't let his hands near, her body already
His shtetl house, his shack in a field.
How soon forgotten the superstition of love,
That faith in one another strong as a God
Not yet jilted by enlightenment,
Electric lamps and diesel trains, Kristallnacht
Like the rite of stomping on a glass
For luck beneath the wedding canopy, forgone
One hasty Saturday for the justice
Of the peace. My father dabbled with the dark side
Just visiting her island, and she wooed him
From their plans, eloped with him across miles
Of temperament, less ethereal than different,
A real live woman. Against her, my grandparents
Didn't have a prayer, espousing a sad mistrust,

Hiding in the ghetto of the past. She said
What he said, bosomed his words in her accent,
A delusion of magic, of something charmed, conspired
From nothing, shawl of tomb dust, blown ash,
Burnt offering of the synagogue the world
Might not dissipate, if they only believed enough.

The Bomber at the Museum

Silver and restrained, a winged monument
Phoenixed from crates of rusty junk, she stands good
As new in her throng of onlookers,
Could rise from her shadow if given the gas.
The sleek lines speak for themselves, *Enola Gay*,
Graffiti on the nose, the cursive
Pilot's mother's name, though a plaque boasts
*Most sophisticated   dropped the first
Used in combat on Hiroshima Japan.*
That and nothing more of the city
Which returned to earth as vaporous dust,
Less easily puzzled together. Nowhere
Does one find my grandfather, a major
During the Occupation, and a doctor,
Who did nothing, all he could, bowing
Over a fisherman called Takumi,
An exhibit of calm intelligence, the ooze
And scent of ruined flesh in that louvered ward,
A true expert of fission among specialists.
The props turn in my mind, the facts reduced
To rivets and metal plate I crouch beneath,
Denial the very thing that hurts most
Those who don't survive, who simply come later.
Memory of a memory, he's phantasmal
As ash, like those silhouettes of disfigured girls
On *This Is Your Life*, the Hibakusha maidens
Who flew to New York in the fifties
For plastic surgeons to revise the event
In their faces. In the studio dark they met
Millions at a distance and a pale sweaty pilot.
He's gone now too, and my grandfather,
Who I resurrect inert as words, an emissary

Like the extra man in the story
Of Shadrach and his companions
In the fiery furnace, the one inexplicably
Among them like a son of God. If I burn now
It is only with shame, the past a crucible
From which I emerge alive if not unscathed.

Golem

Survivor of a bus ride to work that blossomed
Into deafening smoke, a swarm of glass, for him
The sting has passed. It's others who wince
When they meet him, ask if just with their eyes.
He's hideous, has a map of scarred Jerusalem
Clawed across his cheeks, prefers a dark room
Though it's they who speak in anger, assume
He's dumbly strong for them with his visible grudge,
At their command like the golem roaming
The streets of Prague, the Jewish Frankenstein
Who defended his ghetto from the mobs.
But mostly he's sad, can't stand the grotesquerie
That passes for news anymore, the soldiers
Shooting boys, the boys dressed as soldiers
Getting on buses with fulminant belts, sons
Of dirt, of fly-mobbed sheds who have nothing
And so much, the kind of smile that fetches girls.
He's shattered and put back together, less
Than a man though more than legend or clay
In another's hands, has found a soul
Amid all the wreckage. But sometimes, hearing
An ambulance wail its pilgrimage he wonders
If it was a mistake, if God's confused him
With someone else like the schlimazel
In a comedy of errors who goes under
For a gallbladder and wakes with his legs cut off.
When hands begged his away from his mask
Of gauze, he grabbed back hard, had to make them see:
He didn't belong there. But appearances
Held sway, the pretty nurse trying not
To look sickened when they wheeled him in
As if monstrousness really showed in the face.

Photograph of Mass Grave Unearthed, Rwanda

"... after Auschwitz, to write a poem is barbaric"
—Theodor Adorno

It takes a year for a body to purge itself
Down to bones. A photograph never loses
Its soul, interest that fades, memory that suffers
A slow decay, the perpetrators not the only ones
To walk away dusting off their hands. Events
Bury events in a kind of noise, and this picture,
The thousand words it merits, to boast these
As some of those might insinuate the worst
Kind of verse, dumb testimony, faithful observation,
A woman sunlight and film discover kneeling
By the excavated mound. Any attempt
To sing about her would by comparison butcher
The music and rhythm of her wailing, a voice
Still with us, a voice that carries more
Than its weight. So let this poem be
Leaden and prosaic, baggage, brutal even, a hill
Of skulls far from Poland, a different town
But the same woman holding her hair
And opening her mouth. For her there is
No critique with which to counter, no philosophizing
Or thinking out loud, no Orpheus
With his lyre and heavy footsteps
From echo into brilliance, no after.

II

Miners

After Van Gogh
"Surely all art is the result of one's having been
in danger, of having gone through an experi-
ence all the way to the end, where no one can
go any further."
—Rilke

He could have used dirt as his medium,
Even the air a brown weight as they sleepwalk
Past the sullen trees and fuming buildings,
Nothing sketchy, his pencil knowing
With dark dust every inch of them,
A helpless, benevolent witness.
An artist shouldn't preach, or so he hears
Preached to him. But Van Gogh isn't an artist,
Not yet, works for the church, a street minister
Raving as best he can about heaven
To those who spend their lives over their heads
In earth. You'd have to be out of your mind
To descend willingly into their terse hole,
Take the slow fall by creaking winch, reach them
By becoming them, looking up at the bright mote
Of day as at a star. How could he not
Become shrill to the point of beauty,
Which is the breaking point, the collapse
Of reason, granite shuddering away
From the precious lode? It was years before his hands
Began their mission of saffron and starry light,
Gray lines and paper. But these men endure,
Stay with him like silt beneath his fingernails.
In the drawing they've emerged, come to rest;
When he scratches down their clumsy shovels,
Their blank eyes and bowed heads, he's saving them.

The Goose Girl

For Shira

The realist works of Millet grace those
No one dreams becoming, the woodcutter,
The bowed gleaner, the goose girl who never
Budges from her place at the bottom
Of a hill by the mud pond. She leans her cheek
Against her staff in a way that reveals,
More than ennui, that awful, noble patience
With being poor. If she's heard of the traveling
Princess forced to trade clothes with her maid,
She doesn't see how such make-believe pertains,
Has never been anything but a follower
Of birds. The fairy tale is the charade
Of privilege itself, that it ever gets exposed
And set right, the magic in his peasants
Their refusal to show bitterness, disenchantment,
Mistake identity for the coarse fabric
In a shawl, a skirt, a blouse. Unlike her geese,
Their flight feathers culled, she manages to rise
Above the tired narrative while standing
Within its bounds. As for the storytellers,
Their nail-spiked barrel dragged by horses,
Sharp comeuppance for those who deserve it
In the end, Millet, who died penniless, grants her
No such satisfaction, only lack of the need.

Portrait

After Arshile Gorky

She doesn't sit for him but for whoever
Takes her picture, the one from which he woos her,
His mother, ageless and beautiful as paint,
Her babushka a soft, round frame. He stands by
And just beyond her, flowers in his hand,
Though it's his Armenian eyes which hold you,
Sad because they're dark, dark because they're sad.
The same as hers, they stare out and away,
Disavowal which acknowledges the years
That intervene between his shoulders and hers,
Her ample aproned lap. She starved, vanished
In his arms so he could eat, and you might
Call hunger how this has gnawed at him,
How he had to make her out of anything
He could find, even himself. Think of Orpheus
Who can't look and looks anyway, reprising
Those steep miles on foot, the forced road from Khorgum
To Yerevan, the hellish trek reversed,
Over and over, drafts, sketches, oils, *hundreds*
And hundreds of layers to obtain the weight,
Orpheus who wouldn't be denied
Taking a Russian name, the palette
A lyre of soft tones, of vibrant strokes.
He portrayed her so often she sometimes came
To have some other woman's face, missing
Her hands because only the finished
Can die, never abstract no matter
The official stance about "the incident,"
The river's mum litany of corpses. Forget
The facts like bones and the photographs of bones,
Still this, always this, losing her again
So as not to lose her completely.

35

Easter, 1930

It begins with a light rain and a prayer
Of thanks, the ice-edged dawn of a decade,
April outside the church, and the bread line,
No different after the grime of slept-in clothes,
The days-old dinner rolls from restaurants
And Hooverille men no one could remember
In their past lives as grocers and clerks and porters
Before the promise of America became a vow
Of poverty, and they were entered by ghosts.
Eternal as the gaunt gray look of photographs,
Some of them must have had no idea
Just like the disciples when they still had Christ,
When they took him for granted and his miracles
Like the market, the sleight of hand by banks,
The loaves multiplying into fishes, the companies
Enraptured by the Dow, worth nothing to a husband
Without work, a boy without a father. It's all there
In the ledger, on the books, which had closed.
Looking back, it's the worst taste, God,
The life they had, the hopes before it all
Became just bread with maybe a little wine later,
A jug of hooch in the dead-end alley
Between the river and the railroad tracks.
You'd have to be mad like Vallejo in Paris
To appreciate it, to have predicted it for years
With your heart, already suffered it, depression,
The soul's starvation, to have written
Breakfast is drunk down ... Damp earth of the cemetery
Long before this, given everything to the cause
Of your own destruction like those lining up.
But you needn't be him or Christ to rise
While it's dark on yet another day so you can find

A place, to wish you could vanish
In your public shame like a drunk, a hobo,
A suicide, and instead walk home, come back
As more than a bag of bones, the stale bread
Someone hungry might stare at amazed,
Which never lets out its deep breath
But contains what was pent-up and anguished over,
The morning some kind of miracle itself.

Lorca in Harlem, 1929

This man looming against you in the dark
Dying twinkle of late-night uptown
Isn't a fulmination of overflowing rage and want
Expressed in the report of a mugger's pistol,
Just his empty hands confronting your body
With pleasure. He's no one special though good
As anyone, a speakeasy stranger
In the slum's jubilating refuge, powerless
But not silent, embodying the soft moan
Of muffled tremolo from a gin joint,
The free verse of jazz, spirited licks,
A whole other tongue, and is understood.
He's one of your mysterious gypsy songs,
Your lilting letters home, a loose translation
From the Spanish, romance language, the ladies'
Pretty lies, for you his color just one
More prohibition. Soon the thirties will begin
Like a crime spree, encroachment by banks,
Foreclosures by generals, you among the spoils.
Your audience of gun barrels doesn't wait
In a ghetto still known without irony
As Dreamland where you sleep with your wooed shadow,
The dark repressed half of yourself. You must
Return to Spain, archaic nobility, genteel assassins
Who needn't conceal their aims, whose wives
Fancy you stylish for the refined bacchanalia
Of soirees in their interior gardens
But sour in the end, turn on you like wine.

Lorca's Grave

In 1936 they fill a hole with him
No one knows where. Some say this glade
Among the olive trees, the great human dump
Of Barranco de Viznar. But in Spain
Every town has a mass grave, a midden
Of souls, and if at last his bones divulge themselves
They will in that awkward, inarticulate way
Most of us have of putting things. Buried would stay
His lilt, his deep song, mum here as anyplace.
If only the grass and blameless earth could answer
It wouldn't be enough. If he has words left
They fall from your lips. Even in the silence
When you ponder them stark and inert
On a page, you find him, hear his voice
In your head and he lives in the whisper
Of your slow breath. Standing where maybe
He last stood I try to imagine you
And everyone who has ever read him,
Even the forty years of burned books and prison
Under Franco, all those faint provocations
To the air combined, how they remain insubstantial
And inexorable, a gentle breeze
Riffling my hair. I almost have to laugh
At the dictator's thugs that morning,
Themselves at the bottom of the pit
Of the forgotten, in a country steeled
For another gasp, another moan, disdaining
The body whose whereabouts, whose very name
They were about to rescind, shoveling
And sweating, believing their guns had spoken
For the true Spain, that they could bury the wind.

Captain Barros Basto, Apostle of the Marranos

You stormed the 1920s on horseback,
In full uniform, decorated and alone or sometimes
Brought a doctor to perform the circumcisions.
Other than that small sword you assailed no one.
Yet this peasant making dirt cough with his spade
Looks up to stare you down as his ancestors
Might have Torquemada. Devious wolf, he blessed
Any ruse that let him pounce on his swine—
What marrano really meant—forced converts,
Secret Jews consumed with Christ's passion
Or holy fire, whichever came first. You came
To tell their children's children the secret kept
So well it was now lost, let them be
Who they were only more so, a Portuguese man
Of war seeking peace with God through this mission
And bearing gifts, the facts, sacred though hardly
Innocent, which still could sting. The striped white cloth,
The prayers in common, though mispronounced, proved
Only the intricate randomness of devotion
Like the sublime pattern on a butterfly's wings,
A hundred others the same only different
When observed up close, and so he shook his head
Though you raved about the cathedral of the north,
As you called your synagogue built with bricks and spit
And borrowed cash. You died exorcised by your own
And by the church, your dream in ruins, the peasant
Still lighting benighted candles and declining ham
Which changed nothing. A hog would trample
Priceless parchment to get to his trough of slop,
Yet stay pure in the eyes of God, and that part
Where Jesus shoos demons from a man possessed

Into a herd of grunts and curly tails, washed
Away in the sea, well, maybe there was one
He missed. Maybe the devil in the details
Of faith is the soul itself, which doesn't know
It's perverse, only that it calls home this
Modest though sturdy house of skin and bone,
Only that it has to live for no reason
Besides living, like a butterfly or the last,
Cleverest pig who won't be lured or driven out.

Blood of the Beasts

After Georges Fraju

In the ruins of forties Paris, poor children
Hold hands, a lamp hangs suspended like a star
Among the cast-away objects of art,
An umbrella, an old phonograph,
And then the movie cuts away
To the slaughterhouse. You smoke and banter
With others herding in the animals,
Hum as you take the calf in your arms
To slit its throat and I look at you
Like the angel at Abraham. I think
Maybe one of those in the street belongs
To you, that maybe you bedazzle a son
With the same pretty tune putting him to sleep.
Victory maims an apartment house, a small café,
The calm in the narrator's voice almost righteous
Amid the terrified lows, a void
Of feeling to go along with the missing
Fingers in the man standing next to you.
I watch the cows on their hooks fly overhead
As in some sadistic parody of Chagall
Not much else but that glut of sirloin
When you're young and full of no skill
Except a willingness to pare yourself down
To one knife-wielding hand. At night,
Where we can't see, it becomes gentle again,
Touching your wife. Still I wonder about
The numbness that must creep up your forearm
From the hours of slashing, if it penetrates
To your heart, anesthesia like a bolt in the head
The white horse gets as he falls nobly
To his knees, so that you might forget

The difference between what you love
And some pathetic creature. A shot
Of a train evinces other trains
And I think of Chagall's painting of the flayed ox,
His grandfather helpless in one corner, holding
The sacred blade, below him the village
In flames, the closeness of atrocity to ritual,
Dear blood, and I see you as one of my own.

Nijinsky, 1939

Life magazine, the asylum's June-green Alps.
A freeze frame reveals all for all to see
After twenty years, the mad emperor
Of the dance, a bald old man, his back
To the barre, his arms winged out, his feet
Three feet in the air, gray shadow leaping
Above shadow. Stripped of aura, intuition
About these visitors who smile, politely applaud,
He's more naked in his tumid three-piece suit
Than when Rodin had him pose, those thighs
Made of bronze in 1914. No footage exists
To prove his legend unless you imagine
Photographs strung together in animation.
He once bragged his secret, that he leapt
And paused, and here, pitiful in decline
Refuses to fall, hams for the lens, his chin
Held up, his eyes level, oblivious
As those jinxed cartoons who venture off a bluff
Full tilt and plummet to orchestral blare
Only when they look. As for a world
Whose art no longer has rules, whose numbers
Won't admit the meaning of death, people
On the brink flock to movies and in the shorts
Between features, laugh at Elmer Fudd.
Some claim Nijinsky's innovations
An early psychotic hint. But here again
He dances the mocking dream of grace, the lie
That his body rules everywhere it moves,
His whole life one avant-garde performance.
A miracle, the text fawns in that tone
Used with those one wishes kept in the dark.
They come as his own voice, insistent, bold,

Imploring him, the sweet-talking thieves. They come
As the abyss, the part of him that won't die,
Isn't a god. He calls this dancing, and so it is.

Aperture

"The camera ... teaches people
how to see without a camera."
—Dorothea Lange

Wake Island, Corregidor, bombs bursting
Like flashbulbs, the enemy's sun rising
Everywhere, she captures this Japanese
American boy on film the Army impounds
For the threat he poses, arms at his sides,
His uniform a Cub Scout belted blazer
And pants, ready to ship out for the pacific
Deserts of California, Manzanar.
Judging by his patient gaze she mustn't
Scare him either, swiveling the huge Graflex
Like a machine gun on its tripod.
She's ventured white into a sea
Of Asians, but he never finds her
Subversive. The government does, the men
Who hired her just to lower her eyes
To the focusing hood, press the button
For all to see the care with which they took
The things in his life, his friends, his home, his school,
His life. Following orders with too much fidelity,
She includes the prim tie, the designation tag
Pinned like a ribbon, his proud stare. You can't see
Her at all, the marred childhood she tows around
Like a bad leg, the polio she said
Formed her, guided her, humiliated her all at once.
You know her through his glance, his spying
Someone he trusts to command his chin up,
His hands just so. They share a world of difference
From which they can't hide, a sudden breakdown
In the integrity of who they are, fine surrender,
A flaw that admits both sorrow and light.

Cargo Cult

Your father's war stories weighed upon us
That night, but only lightly because we enter
One another's past with such fascination
And distance that the most volatile scenes
Appear placid as if viewed from great altitude.
That is how I pictured his foamy ocean
And his dark green islands of the South Pacific.
Someone more tragically fierce and futile
Than the natives who hunted each other in thongs
And fingerpaint would be hard to imagine
If he hadn't sipped brandy right before us
Describing how everything depended upon
Those volcanic anthills of sand and jungle.
But most absurd, of course, was the misguided
Mysticism of the tribal elders who believed
A cantankerous C-46 was some kind of khaki god
With a belly full of rifles and Army surplus.
Reverent with terror, they prayed for canned corn
And tins of sardines and stuffed themselves
With a holy spirit whose heaven didn't lie
Among stars but in the factories of Michigan
And Illinois, assembling their miracles
In shifts overseen by foremen tough as any emperor
In Tokyo. Yet no icon loomed more overblown
Than your father's C.O. with a thing for
The black angel your father could never save
Even as she saved him from black water fever
And its less discerning ardor. I could see her,
Perhaps a little too close, sitting by his cot
To sponge up his shaking chills and fustian
That meant no less than any other English
While warm air rolled through the infirmary

Like surf. I saw her eyes long clear through
That unstoppable tide for the simple height
In which the cargo planes swooped, teasing
The green swells like gulls, the bed shivering
On its own as they approached. He embraced her
Once but she had long ago turned cynical in more
Disciplined arms. The best he could do was impose
His tags and a small silver crucifix when he left.
Yet I believe salvation at her hands is still proof
Of some kind of primitive and spare divinity
Not quite more than human, which bears us
Up and onwards in spite of ourselves
Like rattling freight, although she might have adjured
Its descent someday to claim all its white souls
Except his in the same wooden crates.

Parable of the Capsized Canoe

For Odette

Bullied by a squall, the pirogue doesn't roll
Completely, though closer than Lewis and Clark
Could want, its sail smashed against the cold boil
Of a spring flush Missouri. Here Sacagawea appears
In the diaries of men who don't think enough
Of her for words more than a few times.
Noting the sudden flotsam of tools, medicines,
The diaries themselves, she reaches out
And grabs what she can. It hardly sounds heroic,
But Lewis writes as though astonished to find her
Equal in fortitude and resolution
With any person on board. This makes her legend
Maybe more a dispelling of myth,
All he never expected of someone
Fine-boned and quiet and with a baby
On her back, pure hyperbole to say
She led him, as in showing how he might come
To the Oregon coast and beyond it
The dark, homely inn on Natchez Trace.
They pointed where, took her hoping only
She might coax horses or at least good will
From her own, suspicious of what men portended
Where they didn't belong, country rough
As much for the sorrow one could raise
In another as for mountains or snowbound woods
Or white water. Maybe this frigid river
Reflects the little she truly was guide to,
Having overturned, so calmly and without fanfare,
What they assumed, bringing them soaked
And trembling to witness her doing
With her small, mysterious life all she could do.

Rushmore

In memory of the activist, Anna Mae
Aquash

They mask what they overlook, the bluffs
Around them, the reservations, Wounded Knee,
Legacy's raw and obdurate terrain.
Once there was a woman; not far, 1970s.
Ninety miles and a nation away,
An early spring unveiled her, hard as sculpture,
Slain under months of snow.

                    Now they've exhumed
Her case, still shaping the truth. Well, it's simple:
There are no human shrines. She drank herself out
Of a smashed marriage, gave breath to songs, some shrill
As Dakota wind, smuggled food through a standoff
With marshals, had a way with children, especially
Her own.

           One might contrast her unfinished work
With that of Gutzon Borglum, worshipful son
Of immigrants, who slowly carved while strung
From a bosun's seat, defaced Red Cloud's Black Hills
Then at the dedication confessed the land
As stolen. He never rendered the "wild and carefree"
Natives, though he yearned to.

                   Some will say who
Knew about the bullet in her head. Some will say
Almost anything, like the FBI whispering
Threats in one ear, bribes in the other,
Who may have used her as an informer
Or hinted that they did.

                 She wasn't Cary Grant's
Impeccable blond, the government spy
He saves in *North by Northwest,* dangling

From the monument while a subversive goon grinds
His hand with a shoe. It was Nixon stepping
On everyone's rights, obsessed with sympathizers,
A cinch to badmouth. But what of Lincoln,
She'd have asked, sad bass of the quartet, the one
With a conscience deep in the monolith, hanging
38 Sioux in Mankato because the settlers whooped
For hundreds, his moonlit cheek a sheer drop?

Maybe one day a repentant artist
Will idolize Leonard Peltier with granite
In the shadow prison a Badlands ridge of pines
Projects at dusk, Russel Means storming Rushmore.
But with Anna, he'll never have a chance.
How does one capture her smile, her daughters
So terribly young? Some people you can't make
Out of stone. Once they're gone, they're gone.

Medusa

All they let you see is her head when you walk
Into the room and gaze through its window
In the wall of another room, your daughter
Already excavated by hands
Of latex and sewn back together, covered,
Out of decorum, the sheet drawn down just enough
To know. You're a man and men are stone
Because they have to be, but in this moment
Stone crumbles; the skin quivers uncontrollably.
It's time which has turned still and hard.

                               How many
Months have you stood in that last look, her
Puffed, distorted face among the clotted locks
Still lovely through the ringing phone's held breath,
The clumsy courtesy of detectives who forgot
To ask some small thing, not used to the delicate
Myth you once called the world?

                              Even his trial
Simply adds to yours, tolerating him
Across the aisle, forced to sit and listen
To his obsessions, which old snapshots transfixed him,
The exact angle he swooped in the knife,
While you imagine her, heroic, petrified,
Unlisted number, one small cave of an apartment
After another. Cold as a statue, cloaking
His smirk with a suit he's worn this once, he still
Won't meet your stare. He can tell but never feel,
Words the cunning shield in which he beholds
Himself while you stroke the dead snakes of her hair.

The Rape of the Sabine Women

Well into her first mile beneath a bridge
She understood his eyes right away,
August, four years ago. The whole time
A stream hid them in its tittering hush. The song
Playing when he tore off her headphones,
She still can't listen to.
                              The others thank her
For sharing, artificial punch already in cups,
Beige light softening the overheated
Third floor of a church, snow padding the sills
Of thick windows. *My own husband,* she confesses,
Doesn't know.
                      Then the kid, Sandy, who scoffs
Most suggestions, wants to barmaid again,
Move on; she has a nose ring, serious makeup,
Carries a gun. Or the conscience, as they call her,
The professor who keeps minutes, everyone
On theme. She shook her head at pictures
In the ER, her case thrown out, corresponds
With someone in Bosnia, the war against her
And the peace, even calm nights like this.

Because you bare them as facts, as yours, I understand
Why Poussin is obscene, the public pleasure
Of museums, Rossetti's Persephone
A bruised pomegranate not a ravishing heroine,
Like the woman who emerges from the hiss
Of the 46 bus and crosses the street,
Running in the midst of her brisk walk.
                                            Blind
Footfall, I want to tell her what I told you
After the concert, when you described what felt good

Actually hurt, that you smelled leaves,
Wet dirt when I held your breast, questioning
If I knew my own past, or my hands
The difference between desire and need, yes
And surrender, *No, no, no, you're wrong*
About me. But she only hears heavy shoes.

III

Slow Dance

In the mist and murk of the dance floor
You swoon against your girl, tense with lust,
Aimless in your spirals as a seed of milkweed
Following the wind like all the others
Who bump you politely with their eyes shut
As though grief-struck or seized with religion
While the band plays one for the road.
Letting yourself see, you zero in on the fated boy
With whom no one dances, his hands hoisting
The tails of his white dinner jacket
From inside the pockets like clipped wings.
When your cat bears its young, he's the last out,
The runt who doesn't get licked, but eaten.
You wonder about his life, if it always goes
Like this or worse, a constant wounding because
Of thick glasses or a growth on his nose,
Until he saddens for himself and sours
On others, wounding them in turn, and how
His sadness might leave him cancer-prone, or lead
To some damnable crime against nature,
The same nature that makes you want so much
To help him. You would gladly lend him the keys
To your convertible, or your lettered cardigan,
Anything to give a girl the wrong impression.
But you know that his best chance at salvation
Might come here and now, if he would only
Twirl and shuffle his feet where the PTA
And the mayor in his mad top hat and the pastor
Representing God in all His infinite mercy
Have ordained. But that would mean forking over
Your flame, the Prussian blonde to whom you've sworn
Your soul, being so young and foolish, the one

You would lord away if he even tried to tap
Her bare shoulder. With a cat's sharp
And slender smile, she might, all too easily,
Glide from her dress so that you would have to
Kill them both or spend eternity cringing
From your shadow. Chosen lightly as a car
Or sweater, random as a seed touching down,
She comes to symbolize this milestone, prom
Or wedding, which in turn evokes the long
Slow song of life itself, and nothing makes you
Quite as selfish, because here you dance
For youth, for love, for all the days you won't.

Fiddle

The endless details which compose a life
Often pass for mere accompaniment
Like the tune which crackles on the radio
Just ahead of news announcing war

Is over or the strains of a jig
Some total stranger croons to my wife
In the pub at 9th and Fitzwater
Our first night out. But one small thing

Leads to another and who can argue
As he saws his fiddle, cradling the hips
Of burnished wood, studying the blur
Of his fingers. He plays beyond himself

Like the rest of us, staking his fate
On each slight movement. One bad slice
Could shred the trance he looms with his upper hand.
Still, we sip our ale, paying attention, destined

To be lovers with only love in common
And priceless like a Stradivarius: grand
For music and not much else. I don't give
An ear to the counterpoint, how we might use

Affection more as weapon than instrument,
Our struggle so much fiddling around
In the greater tumult, one uneven verse
For a mostly sad ballad. I haven't come

To her place in my life as what's tenuous
Instead of her thin waist when I hold her

As if she might not stand my touch.
Maybe years ago I heard it all

But only now do I listen sometimes
As if I'd left the past
Up in the air and could still arrange it
Anyway I like, the high notes and low notes

Into one sweet melody I miss. Perfect
In the sense of gone, its simple rhythm
Won't break down, our integrity hard-pressed
Like the strings, nothing to us but a song.

Expatriate

Seeing you tick across that socialite's veranda
In your heels to say you'd given up the spicy
Telescoped life of a correspondent and greet me
With your husband the surgeon, a silk blazer thrown
Over his blood-stained scrubs for effect, amazed me
More than the news of your death I'd invented
Not knowing better. You kept me honest for years
With your vanishing, your moral delusions
They sometimes published as facts, your certitudes
Arrant upon the commonplace as moonlight sweeping
The landscaped grass. When we last spoke
I knelt over you in your third floor walk-up
And leaned to kiss you in the soft, American
Blindness of a small town whose name doesn't matter.
You would have inveighed anywhere against
The blissful bakery and laundromat, claiming
Revolution lay interred under two centuries,
That you had to rescue Soweto or Chad by way
Of Paris, ignoring my protests over how hard it was
Just to save ourselves. Truth be told, I wanted you
To die for everything you imagined at the edge
Of our facile suffering, your jeep humbled
By plastique on some bridge in Belfast or Beirut,
Some penumbra of our enlightenment, while we
Turned gaunt with crash diets and midlife crises,
Genuflected on hand-picked lawns, squinting
For a contact lens, vicariously absolved.
When you slid off into that fable you always told
About the pity of the world, I'd assumed it would be
For good, staving off the craven sorrow we earn
By living that you now reported would never leave.
Breaking down with a smile, you let your husband

Gently knife a hand through your hair the way
We all dissect complicity from complacency.
In the dark long ago where I barely made out
Your eyes, your mouth, I took your words
At face value. You spoke of an undiscovered America,
A sudden place, a country barely on earth.
That night you built a bridge there between us
With your young unselfish body and I believed
Too much in all you stood for. More than justice,
I miss that zeal and pleasure, as if you were
Your own rhetoric or land of exile whose soil
I would have dropped to my knees and kissed
More often, had I known I was never coming back.

Groundless and Still Believed

When Flight 103 turned into a Roman candle
High over Scotland I sat caught up
Somewhere in the nonstop transit of my life
And let it pass. I didn't know that someday
I'd know Katy, who heard as she got off work
Stubbing tickets at an O'Hare flight gate
Where she'd often dreamed of flitting wasp-thin
Up that sublime aisle of stares and elbows
With a Mae West or more coffee. I didn't know
The shrugged off husks of all those lives
Would matter so much because one woman never
Quite shed enough to rise back into herself
After she tore off her regulation skirt and shoes
For good and frittered them on her floors
Like an aileron or maybe half a rudder
Startling a sheep field. She plunged face down
On her bed and like gleaming litter broke up
Over a pilot she'd joked with once or twice.
There, with the same window open and the same
Neighbor's porch light busy with moths
Like some lackluster beacon for life and the way
It muddles on, I could finally comfort her.
It's as if the lonely truth were dead weight
One must avoid at all costs like those fearless
Inventors of flying machines. I didn't care
If she felt dishonest to survive untouched
When she felt the breeze caress her bare length
And decided it was good, and denied the rest.
Crickets drained the sorrow in that white China
Bowl of a moon, keening through clipped wings
And very much alive somewhere in the damp grass.
She'd hardly lost anyone, but knowing him

Let all those others come down on her so hard
From the thin air of whatever mild future
She'd imagined, that on that first night
We made love she had to cry first and tell me.
Perhaps when my hands began to lighten her
Of her clothes she thought I might suspend
Her disbelief, that she might drift away, content,
Into the known world and its illusions, accessible
Only by some delicate and unnatural act
Of faith, like a man with a harness and two wisps
Of fabric leaping from a cliff or twenty tons
Of rubber, glass, and metal rising against
Common sense—that by now she should know better.

Magic

She wanted more out of life
Than her father could give, more
Than the thick knobs of his hands, more
Than his breath of warm stout, more
Than one room and three sisters
With whom she shared it, more
Than how he died: a fireman, but not
In a burning house. Cancer drew him
Over its own slow coals. She wanted
Paris, a husband with ambition —
Maybe a surgeon — enlightened children,
Magic.

Other times she grew wistful
Fanning out a stack of Polaroids
Like a deck of cards
To pick as if by sleight of hand
The one some stranger snapped
The night her father pulled a small girl
Pale as a rabbit from the flames.
He stood for the flash as he always stood
In life, blackened and amazed
Like some stage magician
Whose trick had exploded harmlessly
In his face. It was then
That her heart understood
What it could not understand—
An illusion so grand it mystifies
Even the wiliest conjuror or physician.

Glass

The wineglass your wife surrenders with a soft *oh*
At a friend's gallery reception, lets fall
On the polished slate tile while talking
With her effusive hands, serves not as omen
But reminder of your separation months ago.

Slightly smashed yourself, you find the sound
Of dispersing crystal faintly mellifluous
Like someone standing at a distance
From the pealing carillon of a church.

You watch one of the men in her circle
Of admirers bend with her towards the glitter
And hate how even her clumsiness beguiles,
Both of them laughing with surprise at the pearl
Of blood he licks from a finger.
                                    Too much
Merlot and you stare at how she fills the goblet
Of her dress, your thoughts a million fragments
Of confusion as you remember the thin, sweet taste
Of her mouth. But swaying over stone,
You recall her sharp edges, your passion
As anger, all that keeps you apart, haphazardly
Distinct, still capable of a perfect fit
Like pieces of a broken thing.

Tolerance

Boasting after a wedding and her third
Mai Tai that he hadn't touched her even once
In twenty years, she means no fat lip,
No cigarette brand stubbed in her arm
By a man also drunk and at your table
Where mingle the various social ranks.
You pity her for her fulfillment
Of your lurid expectations, the pink rose
Etched on her shoulder, the impasto makeup,
How the others sneak out that thin smile
Tantamount to rolling the eyes, just more refined,
Reserved for those who exult in what is
Too basic to mention. Her husband tells you
Nothing about his shop, not really his,
What he made there or how much he made for it,
Only that he's felt like smacking her
A few times, and grins. But maybe you know
Enough about lathes or saws or drills
Even if you've never assailed metal
In order to live, a motor in pieces
Like treasure, the shriek of a bearing ground true.
Maybe you know about tolerance, what it means,
A thousandth of an inch all the difference
Amid miles of pounding friction. Or maybe
You don't, but can guess—empathy, common sense—
What it's like, soggy shirt sticking as one powerful arm
Feeds and the other twists the handwheel, steady,
Machine-like, all day, every day, how machines build
Up heat with use, belts wear thin, bolts snap,
How he's reached out, a blur coming close to her
Loud eyes, hard mouth, no one exempt, children
Scattering like the shop's shining detritus.

Maybe once or twice you've had a job
Paid by the hour you thought wouldn't end
Even as the years passed others by, so your lips
Don't curl even as you understand commitment
Takes more than stopping the hands one is good with
A hair's breadth from the face, more than your own
Poor effort to demonstrate or at least explain,
How close is close and never is still never.

About the Author

David N. Moolten is the author of two previous books of poetry, *Plums & Ashes* (Northeastern University, 1994), which won the Samuel French Morse Poetry Prize, and *Especially Then* (David Robert Books, 2005). His verse has been widely published and anthologized. A physician specializing in transfusion medicine, Dr. Moolten was educated at Harvard College and the University of Pennsylvania School of Medicine. He lives, writes, and practices medicine in Philadelphia, Pennsylvania.